Plain English for Lawyers

Plain English
for
Lawyers

RICHARD C. WYDICK

Carolina Academic Press
Durham, North Carolina
1979

To JJW, with love.

L.C.C. Card No. 79-53956
ISBN: 0-89089-175-3 (paper)
ISBN: 0-89089-176-1 (cloth)

Carolina Academic Press
P.O. Box 8791, Forest Hills Station
Durham, North Carolina 27707
Printed in the United States of America.

TABLE OF CONTENTS

Acknowledgements

This book is an expanded and revised version of an article which originally appeared in 66 California Law Review 727, published by the students of the University of California, Berkeley, School of Law, copyright 1978, California Law Review, Inc.

The author wishes to thank Brian E. Gray for his editorial work and to thank Ralph C. Taylor, John L. Vohs, Max Byrd, and Richard Haas for their critical comments. The author also wishes to thank Deena G. Peterson and Ronald R. McClain for their research on sexism in legal writing.

Richard C. Wydick
Davis, California
July, 1979

Chapter One—Why Plain English?

We lawyers cannot write plain English. We use eight
words to say what could be said in two. We use old,
arcane phrases to express commonplace ideas. Seeking
to be precise, we become redundant. Seeking to be cautious, we become verbose. Our sentences twist on, phrase
within clause within clause, glazing the eyes and numb-
ing the minds of our readers. The result is a writing style
that has, according to one critic, four outstanding char-
acteristics. It is: "(1) wordy, (2) unclear, (3) pompous,
and (4) dull."[1]

Criticism of lawyers' writing is nothing new. In 1596
an English chancellor decided to make an example of a
particularly prolix document filed in his court. The
chancellor first ordered a hole cut through the center of
the document, all 120 pages of it. Then he ordered that
the person who wrote it should have his head stuffed
through the hole, and the unfortunate fellow was led
around to be exhibited to all those attending court at
Westminster Hall.[2]

When the common law was transplanted to America,
the writing style of the old English lawyers came with it.

---

1. D. MELLINKOFF, THE LANGUAGE OF THE LAW 24 (1963).

2. Mylward v. Welden (Ch. 1596), *reprinted in* C. MONRO,
ACTA CANCELLARIAE 692 (1847).

In 1817 Thomas Jefferson lamented that in drafting statutes his fellow lawyers were accustomed to "making every other word a 'said' or 'aforesaid,' and saying everything over two or three times, so that nobody but we of the craft can untwist the diction, and find out what it means. . . . "[3]

In recent times criticism of lawyers' writing has taken on a new intensity. The popular press castigates lawyers for the "frustration, outrage, or despair" a consumer feels when trying to puzzle through an insurance policy or installment loan agreement.[4] President Carter has ordered that new regulations of the federal executive agencies must be "written in plain English" that is "understandable to those who must comply" with them.[5] A New York State statute now requires consumer contracts to be written "in a clear and cogent manner using words with common and everyday meanings."[6] Within the legal profession itself, the criticism has mounted. Attorney Ronald Goldfarb charges that, by writing as we do, we "unnecessarily mystify our work, baffle our clients, and alienate the public. We could change this, and we should."[7] The need for change is magnified by

3. Letter to Joseph C. Cabell (September 9, 1817), *reprinted in* 17 WRITINGS OF THOMAS JEFFERSON 417–18 (A. Bergh ed. 1907).

4. Nader, *Gobbledygook,* LADIES' HOME JOURNAL, Sept. 1977, at 68; *see also* TIME, Jan. 16, 1978, at 60; L.A. Times, Jan. 29, 1978, § 1, at 2, col. 5; Wall St. J., Dec. 5, 1977, at 40, col. 1.

5. Exec. Order No. 12044, 43 Fed. Reg. 12,661 (1978).

6. N.Y. GEN. OBLIG. LAW § 5–701b (McKinney 1978).

7. Goldfarb, *Lawyer Language,* LITIGATION, Summer 1977, at 3; *see also* R. LEFLAR, INTERNAL OPERATING PROCEDURES OF APPELLATE COURTS 42–52 (1976).

innovations in the mechanics of lawyering. We now have word processing machines that can type old boilerplate at a thousand words per minute and computer research systems that can give us an instant concordance of all the outpourings of appellate courts, legislatures, and governmental agencies. Soon we may drown in our own bad prose.

A well-known New York lawyer tells the young associates in his firm that good legal writing does not sound as though it had been written by a lawyer. In short, good legal writing is plain English. Here is an example of plain English, the statement of facts from the majority opinion in *Palsgraf v. Long Island Railroad Co.*,[8] written by Benjamin Cardozo:

> Plaintiff was standing on a platform of defendant's railroad after buying a ticket to go to Rockaway Beach. A train stopped at the station, bound for another place. Two men ran forward to catch it. One of the men reached the platform of the car without mishap, though the train was already moving. The other man, carrying a package, jumped aboard the car, but seemed unsteady as if about to fall. A guard on the car, who had held the door open, reached forward to help him in, and another guard on the platform pushed him from behind. In this act, the package was dislodged and fell upon the rails. It was a package of small size, about fifteen inches long, and was covered by a newspaper. In fact it contained fireworks, but there was nothing in its appearance to give notice of its contents. The fireworks when they fell exploded. The shock of the explosion threw down

8. 248 N.Y. 339, 162 N.E. 99 (1928).

some scales at the other end of the platform many feet away. The scales struck the plaintiff, causing injuries for which she sues.

What distinguishes Justice Cardozo's style from that found in most legal writing? Notice his economy of words. He does not say "*despite the fact that* the train was already moving"—he says "*though* the train was already moving." Notice his choice of words. There are no archaic lawyerly phrases, no misty abstractions, no *hereinbefore's*. Notice his care in arranging words. There are no wide gaps between the subjects and their verbs or between the verbs and their objects, and there are no ambiguities to leave us wondering who did what to whom. Notice his use of verbs. Most of them are in simple form, and all but two are in the active voice. Notice the length and construction of his sentences. Most of them contain only one main thought, and they vary in length: the shortest is six words, and the longest is twenty-seven words.

These and other elements of plain English style are discussed in this book. But you cannot learn to write plain English by reading a book. You must put your own pencil to paper. That is why practice exercises are included at the end of each section. When you finish the section, work the exercises and compare your results with those suggested in the back, pages 67-71.

Chapter Two—Omit Surplus Words

As a beginning lawyer, I was assigned to assist an older man, a business litigator. He hated verbosity. When I would bring him what I thought was a finished piece of writing, he would read it quietly and take out his pen. As I watched over his shoulder, he would strike out whole lines, turn clauses into phrases, and turn phrases into single words. One day at lunch I asked him how he did it. He shrugged and said: "It's not hard—just omit the surplus words."

A. How to Spot Bad Construction

In every English sentence are two kinds of words: working words and glue words. The working words carry the meaning of the sentence. In the preceding sentence the working words are these: *working, words, carry, meaning,* and *sentence.* The others are glue words: *the, the, of,* and *the.* The glue words do serve a purpose; they hold the working words together to form a proper English sentence. But when you find too many glue words, it is a sign that the sentence is badly constructed. A good sentence is like fine cabinetwork: the pieces are cut and shaped to fit together with scarcely any glue. When you find too many glue words in a sentence, take it apart and reshape the pieces to fit tighter. Consider this example:

A trial by jury was requested by the defendant.

If the working words are circled the sentence looks like this:

A (trial) by (jury) was (requested) by the (defendant.)

Five words in that nine word sentence are glue: *a, by, was, by,* and *the.*

How can we say the same thing in a tighter sentence with less glue? First, move *defendant* to the front and make it the subject of the sentence. Second, use *jury trial* in place of *trial by jury.* The sentence would thus read:

The defendant requested a jury trial.

If the working words are circled, the rewritten sentence looks like this:

The (defendant) (requested) a (jury) (trial.)

Again there are four working words, but the glue words have been cut from five to two. The sentence means the same as the original, but it is tighter and one-third shorter.

Here is another example:

The ruling by the trial judge was prejudicial error for the reason that it cut off cross-examination with respect to issues which were vital.

If the working words are circled, we have:

The (ruling) by the (trial) (judge) was (prejudicial) (error) for the (reason) that it (cut) (off) (cross-examination) with respect to (issues) which were (vital.)

In a sentence of twenty-four words, eleven carry the meaning and thirteen are glue.

Note the string of words *the ruling by the trial judge.* That tells us that it was the trial judge's ruling. Why not just say *the trial judge's ruling?* The same treatment will tighten up the words at the end of the sentence. *Issues which were vital* tells us they were vital issues. Why not say *vital issues?* Now note the phrase *for the reason that.* Does it say any more than *because?* If not, we can use one word in place of four. Likewise, *with respect to* can be reduced to *on.* Rewritten, the sentence looks like this:

> The trial judge's ruling was prejudicial error because it cut off cross-examination on vital issues.

Here it is with the working words circled:

> The (trial)(judge's)(ruling) was (prejudicial)(error)(because) it (cut)(off)(cross-examination) on (vital)(issues.)

The revised sentence uses fifteen words in place of the original twenty-four, and eleven of the fifteen are working words. The sentence is both tighter and stronger than the original.

Consider a third example, but this time use a pencil and paper to rewrite the sentence yourself.

> In many instances, insofar as the jurors are concerned, the jury instructions are not understandable because they are too poorly written.

Does your sentence trim the phrase *in many instances?* Here the single word *often* will suffice. Does your sentence omit the phrase *insofar as the jurors are concerned?* That adds bulk but no meaning. Finally, did you find a way to omit the clumsy *because* clause at the end of the sentence? Your rewritten sentence should look something like this:

> Often jury instructions are too poorly written for the jurors to understand.

Here it is with the working words circled:

Often jury instructions are too poorly written for the jurors to understand.

The rewritten sentence is nine words shorter than the original, and nine of its twelve words are working words.

Exercise 1

Circle the working words in the sentence below. Compare their number with the number of glue words. Then rewrite the sentence, circle the working words, and compare the result with the original.

In the event that there is a waiver of the attorney-client privilege by the client, the letters must be produced by the attorney for the purpose of inspection by the adversary party.

Compare your answer with the one on page 67. More exercises are on page 73.

B. Avoid Compound Prepositions

Compound prepositions and their close cousins are a fertile source of surplus words. They use several words to do the work of one or two, and they suck the vital juices from your writing. You saw some examples in the last section. *With respect to* was used instead of *on*. *For the reason that* was used instead of *because*.

Every time you see one of these pests on your page, swat it. Use a simple form instead. Here is a list of common ones:

Compound	Simple
at that point in time	then
by means of	by
by reason of	because of
by virtue of	by, under

for the purpose of	to
for the reason that	because
from the point of view	from, for
in accordance with	by, under
inasmuch as	since
in connection with	with, about, concerning
in favor of	for
in order to	to
in relation to	about, concerning
in terms of	in
in the event that	if
in the nature of	like
on the basis of	by, from
prior to	before
subsequent to	after
with a view to	to
with reference to	about, concerning
with regard to	about, concerning
with respect to	on, about

Exercise 2

Use one or two words to replace the compound constructions in these sentences.

a. In the event of the tenant's default, the lease will terminate.

b. From the point of view of simplicity, an ordinary deed of trust would be the best.

c. Prior to the enactment of the statute, the clause was added for the reason that the *Burke* decision seemed to require it.

d. Plaintiff's brief contains several misstatements with respect to the disputed time sequence.

e. When the funds are received, we will transfer title with a view to clearing up all questions in reference to this matter.

f. At this point in time, the witness cannot recall what the letter was with reference to.

Compare your answers with those suggested on page 67. More exercises are on pages 73-74.

C. Trim Out Verbose Word Clusters

Once you develop a dislike for surplus words, you will find many common word clusters that can be trimmed from your sentences with no loss of meaning. Consider this example:

The fact that the defendant was young may have influenced the jury.

What meaning does *the fact that* add? Why not say:

The defendant's youth may have influenced the jury.

The fact that is almost always surplus. See how it can be trimmed from these examples.

Verbose	*Plain*
the fact that she had died	her death
he was aware of the fact that	he knew that
despite the fact that	although, even though
because of the fact that	because

Likewise, the words *case* and *instance* spawn verbosity:

Verbose	*Plain*
in some instances the parties can	sometimes the parties can

in many cases you will find	often you will find
that was an instance in which the court	there the court
discrimination claims are more frequent than was formerly the case	discrimination clauses are more frequent now
injunctive relief is required in the case of	injunctive relief is required when
in the majority of instances the landowner has	usually the landowner
it is not the case that she wrote the letter	she did not write the letter

Here are other examples of common word clusters you can eliminate with no loss of meaning:

Verbose	*Plain*
during the time that	during, while
for the period of	for
in accordance with	by, under
insofar as . . . is concerned	(omit it entirely and start with the subject)
there is no doubt but that	doubtless, no doubt
the question as to whether	whether, the question whether
this is a topic that until	this topic
until such time as	until

Exercise 3

Trim out the verbose word clusters in these examples.

a. At such time as the judgment is entered. . . .

b. This is an instance in which estoppel can be invoked. . . .

c. He was sentenced for a period of five months. . . .

d. Pursuant to the terms of our contract. . . .

e. There can be no doubt but that the statute applies where. . . .

f. The claim was clarified by means of a bill of particulars. . . .

g. The trial judge must consider the question as to whether. . . .

h. This offer will stand until such time as you. . . .

i. In accordance with § 103(b), you are entitled. . . .

j. In most instances good faith is not disputed. . . .

k. The plaintiff filed suit despite the fact that she knew that. . . .

l. Arbitration is useful in some instances where the parties. . . .

m. This is a point that has troubled many courts. . . .

n. Because of the fact that he was injured. . . .

o. The question as to whether there was negligence. . . .

Compare your answers with those suggested on pages 67-68. More exercises are on pages 74-75.

D. How to Shorten Clauses and Phrases

One remedy for rambling sentences is to cut clauses down to phrases. Here is an example:

While the trial was in progress, the judge excluded photographers from the courtroom.

The six word clause at the beginning can be cut to a three word phrase:

During the trial, the judge excluded photographers from the courtroom.

The words *which, who,* and *that* often signal an opportunity to reduce a clause to a phrase:

Clause	Plain
The question was designed to impeach the prosecution witness who had been convicted of having committed a felony.	The question was designed to impeach the prosecution witness, a convicted felon.
The statute, which had been enacted after the *Alyeska* case, authorized the fee award.	The statute, enacted after the *Alyeska* case, authorized the fee award.
The title search did not disclose the easement that had been granted six years before.	The title search did not disclose the easement granted six years before.

When you see the words *it is* and *there are,* stop to see if you can replace a clause by a shorter construction:

Verbose	Plain
There are three key paragraphs in the pretrial order.	The pretrial order has three key paragraphs.

It is possible for the court to take judicial notice of its own own records.	The court can take judicial notice of its own records.
Despite the legislative history, there are doubts about the intent of Congress.	Despite the legislative history, the intent of Congress is in doubt.

Sometimes you can clean out surplus words by replacing a clause with an adjective or adverb:

Verbose	*Plain*
The trial judge denied the defendant's motion, which asked for summary judgment.	The trial judge denied the defendant's summary judgment motion.
The plaintiff rejected the offer made by the defendant to settle the case for $10,000.	The plaintiff rejected the defendant's $10,000 settlement offer.
The decree which was entered in January ordered payments to be made each month for child support.	The January decree ordered monthly child support payments.

Exercise 4

Cut the surplus words from these sentences by shortening clauses and phrases.

    a.   There are three misstatements of fact in appellant's opening brief.

b. The decree which was entered by the lower court does not affect the claim that has been made by the stockholders.

c. It is not necessary for the witness to sign the deposition transcript until the errors that were made by the reporter are corrected.

d. In approving a class action settlement, it is imperative for the court to guard the interests of class members who are not present.

e. There is nothing to tell us whether this misconduct on the part of counsel influenced the verdict rendered by the jury.

f. The agreement with respect to partition that was reached between Smith and Hagen was superseded by the decree that was entered by the court at a later time.

Compare your answers with those suggested on page 68. More exercises are on pages 75-76.

E. Do Not Use Redundant Legal Phrases

Why do lawyers use the term *null and void?* According to the dictionary, either *null* or *void* by itself would do the job. But the lawyer's pen seems impelled to write *null and void,* as though driven by primordial instinct. An occasional lawyer, perhaps believing that *null and void* looks naked by itself, will write *totally null and void,* or perhaps *totally null and void and of no further force or effect whatsoever.*

Null and void is a lawyer's tautology—a needless string of words with the same or nearly the same meaning. Here are other common examples:

alter or change

cease and desist

confessed and acknowledged

last will and testament

made and entered into

order and direct

convey, transfer, and set over	perform and discharge
for and during the period	rest, residue, and remainder
force and effect	save and except
free and clear	suffer or permit
full and complete	true and correct
give, devise, and bequeath	undertake and agree
good and sufficient	unless and until
kind and character	

Lawyer's tautologies have ancient roots. Professor Mellinkoff explains[9] that, at several points in history, the English and their lawyers had two languages to choose from: first, a choice between the language of the Celts and that of their Anglo-Saxon conquerors; later, a choice between English and Latin; and later still, a choice between English and French. Lawyers started using a word from each language, joined in a pair, to express a single meaning. (For example, *free and clear* comes from the Old English *freo* and the Old French *cler*.) This redundant doubling was used sometimes for clarity, sometimes for emphasis, and sometimes just because it was the fashion. Doubling became traditional in legal language and persisted long after any practical purpose was dead.

Ask a modern lawyer why he or she uses a term like *suffer or permit* in a simple real estate lease. The first answer likely will be: "for precision." True, there is a

---

9. D. MELLINKOFF, *supra* note 1, at 38–39, 121–22.

small difference in meaning between *suffer* and its companion *permit*. But *suffer* in this sense is now rare in ordinary usage, and *permit* would do the job if it were used alone.

The lawyer might then tell you that *suffer or permit* is better because it is a traditional legal term of art. Traditional it may be, but a term of art it is not. A term of art is a short expression that (a) conveys a fairly well-agreed meaning, and (b) saves the many words that would otherwise be needed to convey that meaning. *Suffer or permit* fails to satisfy the second condition, and perhaps the first as well. The word *hearsay* is an example of a true term of art. First, its core meaning is fairly well-agreed in modern evidence law, although its meaning at the margin has always inspired scholarly debate.[10] Second, *hearsay* enables a lawyer to use one word instead of many to say that a statement is being offered into evidence to prove that what it asserts is true, and that the statement is not one made by the declarant while testifying at the trial or hearing. Any word that can say all that deserves our praise and deference. But *suffer or permit* does not.

In truth, *suffer or permit* probably found its way into that real estate lease because the lawyer was working from a form that had been used around the office for years. The author of the form, perhaps long dead, probably worked from some even older form that might, in turn, have been inspired by a formbook or some now defunct appellate case where the phrase was used but not examined.

10. *Compare* FED. R. EVID. 801(c) *and* CAL. EVID. CODE § 1200 (West 1966) *with* C. McCORMICK, HANDBOOK OF THE LAW OF EVIDENCE § 246 (2d ed. E. Cleary 1972).

If you want your legal writing to have a musty, form-book smell, by all means use as many tautological phrases as you can find. If you want it to be crisp, do not use any. When one looms up on your page, stop to see if one of the several words, or perhaps a fresh word, will carry your intended meaning. You will find, for example, that the phrase *last will and testament* can be replaced by the single word *will*.[11]

This is not as simple as it sounds. Lawyers are busy, cautious people. The redundant phrase has worked in the past; a new one might somehow raise a question. To check it in the law library will take some time. But remember—once you slay one of these old monsters, it will stay dead for the rest of your career. If your memory is short, keep a card file of slain redundancies. Such trophies distinguish a lawyer from a scrivener.

Exercise 5

In the following passage you will find all the kinds of surplus words described in Chapter Two. Rewrite the passage, omitting as many surplus words as you can.

We turn now to the request which has been made by the plaintiff for the issuance of injunctive relief. With respect to this request, the argument has been made by the defendant that injunctive relief is not necessary because of the fact that the exclusionary clause is

11. Historically, *will* referred to the disposition of realty and *testament* to personalty. *See* W. PAGE, WILLS § 1.3 (Bowe-Parker rev. ed. 1960). Today, *will* suffices for both realty and personalty. *See, e.g.,* CAL. PROB. CODE § 20 (West Supp. 1978).

already null and void by reason of the prior order and direction of this court. This being the case, the exclusionary clause can have no further force or effect, and the defendant argues that in such an instance full and complete relief can be given without the issuance of an injunction. We find ourselves in agreement with this argument.

Compare your answers with those suggested on page 68. More exercises are on page 75.

Chapter Three—Use Familiar, Concrete Words

Here are two ways a lawyer might write to a client to explain why the lawyer's bill is higher than the client expects.

Example One: The statement for professional services which you will find enclosed herewith is, in all likelihood, somewhat in excess of your expectations. In the circumstances, I believe it is appropriate for me to avail myself of this opportunity to provide you with an explanation of the causes therefor. It is my considered judgment that three factors are responsible for this development. Primary among them is the mutually unanticipated expenditure of time which is being necessitated by the litigation involved herein. To wit, the counsel retained on behalf of the several parties defendant is endeavoring, perhaps *in emulationem vicini,* to effect depletion of our resources and destruction of our morale by undertaking deposition proceedings with the purpose of obtaining testimony from numerous deponents whose factual knowledge with respect to the instant litigation is negligible at best. . . .

Example Two: The bill I am sending you with this letter is probably higher than you expected, and I would like to explain the three reasons why. First, the case is taking more time than either you or I expected. The defendants' lawyer, perhaps driven by spite, is trying to wear us down by taking the pretrial testimony of many persons who know little, if anything, about the facts. . .

Example Two is better, is it not? Look at the choice of words in Example One. Why does it author say *statement for professional services* instead of *bill?* The client calls it a bill. So does the lawyer, usually. By tradition, the bill itself can be captioned *statement for professional services.* But this is supposed to be a friendly, candid letter to a client; let us call a bill *a bill.*

Look at the words that give Example One the stink of old law books: *herewith, therefor, herein, several parties defendant, to wit,* and *in emulationem vicini.* None of them is necessary here, if indeed they are necessary at all in a modern lawyer's vocabulary. Look at the airy, abstract words: *circumstances, factors, development.* What do they add here? Finally, look at the number of times Example One uses ponderous phrases instead of the familiar, simple words used in Example Two:

Example One	*Example Two*
in all likelihood	probably
in excess of your expectations	higher than you expected
explanation of the causes	explain why
mutually unanticipated expenditure of time	more time than you or I expected
counsel retained on behalf of the several parties defendant	defendant's lawyer
endeavoring to effect depletion of our resources and destruction of our morale	trying to wear us down

| numerous deponents | many persons |
| factual knowledge . . . is negligible | know little, if anything |

A. Use Concrete Words

To grip and move your reader's mind, use concrete words, not abstractions. To see the difference, suppose that Moses's plagues on Egypt had been described in the language of a modern environmental impact report:

| *Exodus 8:7* | *Altered Version* |
| [A]s the Lord commanded . . . he lifted up the rod and smote the waters of the river . . . and all the waters that were in the river were turned to blood. And the fish that were in the river died; and the river stank, and the Egyptians could not drink the waters of the river; and there was blood throughout all the land of Egypt. | In accordance with the directive theretofore received from higher authority, he caused the implement to come into contact with the water, whereupon a polluting effect was perceived. The consequent toxification reduced the conditions necessary for the sustenance of the indigenous population of aquatic vertebrates below the level of con-tinued viability. Olfactory discomfort standards were substantially exceeded, and potability declined. Social, economic and political disorientation were experienced to an unprecedented degree. |

The lure of abstract words is strong for lawyers. Lawyers want to be cautious and to cover every possibility, while leaving room to wiggle out if necessary. The vagueness of abstract words therefore seem attractive. Particularly attractive are words like *basis, situation, consideration, facet, character, factor, degree, aspect,* and *circumstances:*

> In our present circumstances, the budgetary aspect is
> a factor which must be taken into consideration to a
> greater degree.

Perhaps that means "now we must think more about money," but the meaning is a shadow in the fog of abstract words.

Do not mistake abstraction of that sort for the intentional, artful vagueness sometimes required in legal writing. For example, judicial opinions sometimes use an intentionally vague phrase to provide a general compass heading when it is not possible to map the trail in detail. In *Bates v. State Bar of Arizona*[12] the Supreme Court announced that lawyer advertising is protected by the free speech clause of the first amendment. The Court wanted to tell the states that they could regulate lawyer advertising some, but not too much. The Court could not then tell how much would be too much, so it said that states may impose "*reasonable restrictions* on the time, place and manner" of lawyer advertising.[13] The phrase is intentionally vague. It gives general guidance, but it postpones specific guidance until specific facts come before the Court in later cases. Intentional vagueness is

12. 433 U.S. 350 (1977).
13. *Id.* at 384 (emphasis added).

likewise used in drafting statutes, contracts, and the like, when the drafter cannot foresee every specific set of facts that may arise. But vagueness is a virtue only if it is both necessary and intentional. Knowing when to be vague and when to press for more concrete terms is part of the art of lawyering.

B. Use Familiar Words

Aristotle put the case for familiar words this way: "Style to be good must be clear, as is proved by the fact that speech which fails to convey a plain meaning will fail to do just what speech has to do. . . . Clearness is secured by using the words . . . that are current and ordinary."[14] Given a choice between a familiar word and one that will send your reader groping for the dictionary, use the familiar word. The reader's attention is a precious commodity, and you cannot afford to waste it by creating your own distractions.

Unlike many kinds of writers, attorneys usually know who their readers will be, and their choice of words can be tailored accordingly. A patent lawyer who is writing a brief to be filed in the United States Court of Customs and Patent Appeals can use words that would be perplexing if used in a letter to the inventor-client. Conversely, in writing to the inventor-client, the patent lawyer might use words that would be gibberish if used in a legal brief. In either case, the convenience of the reader must take precedence over the self-gratification of the writer.

14. ARISTOTLE, *Rhetoric* 1404b, in 11 THE WORKS OF ARISTOTLE (W. Ross ed. 1946).

Even among the familiar words, prefer the simple to the stuffy. Don't say *termination* if *end* will do as well. Don't use *expedite* for *hurry,* or *elucidate* for *explain,* or *utilize* for *use.* Do not conclude from this that your vocabulary should shrink to preschool size. If an unfamiliar word is fresh and fits your need better than any other, use it—but don't *utilize* it.

Exercise 6

Rewrite these sentences using familiar, concrete words.
  a. The firmamental hemisphere is undergoing precipitant altitudinal decline.
  b. The prisoner's aptitude for acclimatization to lack of confinement is one factor which must be taken into account in the deliberations of the Parole Board.
  c. The effectuation of reformation of penal institutions is dependent to some degree upon the extent of awareness of current events in that sector among members of the general populace.

Compare your answers with those suggested on pages 68-69. More exercises are on pages 76-77.

C. Do Not Use Lawyerisms

Lawyerisms are words like *aforementioned, whereas, res gestae,* and *hereinafter.* They give writing a legal smell, but they carry little or no legal substance. When they are used in writing addressed to non-lawyers, they baffle and annoy. When used in other legal writing, they give a false sense of precision and sometimes obscure a dangerous gap in analysis.

A lawyer's words should not differ without reason from the words used in ordinary English. Sometimes there is a reason. For example, the Latin phrase *res ipsa loquitur* has become a term of art[15] that lawyers use to communicate among themselves, conveniently and with a fair degree of precision, about a tort law doctrine.[16] But too often lawyers use Latin or archaic English phrases where there is no need. Sometimes they do it out of habit or haste—the old phrase is the one they learned in law school, and they have never taken time to question its use. Other times they do it believing mistakenly that the old phrase's meaning cannot be expressed in ordinary English, or that the old phrase is somehow more precise than ordinary English.

Consider, for example, the word *said* in its archaic use as an adjective. No lawyer in dinner table conversation says: "the green beans are excellent; please pass said green beans." Yet legal pleadings come out like this:

> The object of said conspiracy among said defendants was to fix said retail prices of said products throughout said State of New York.

Lawyers who have an affinity for *said* claim it is more precise than ordinary words like *the,* or *this,* or *those.* They say it means "the exact same one mentioned above." But the extra precision is either illusory or unnecessary, as the example above shows. If only one conspiracy has been mentioned in the preceding material, there is no danger of our mistaking *this* conspiracy for some other conspiracy, and *said* is unnecessary. If more

15. *See* page 19, *supra.*
16. *See* RESTATEMENT (SECOND) OF TORTS § 328 D, comments *a* and *b* (1965).

than one conspiracy has been previously mentioned, *said* does not tell us which of the several is meant. The extra precision is thus illusory. If *the* were put in place of all the *said's,* the sentence would be no less precise and much less clumsy.

Aforementioned is *said's* big brother, and it is just as useless. "The fifty acre plot aforementioned shall be divided. . . ." If only one fifty acre plot has been mentioned before, then *aforementioned* is unnecessary, and if more than one fifty acre plot has been mentioned before, then *aforementioned* is imprecise. When precision is important, use a specific reference: "The fifty acre plot described in paragraph 2(f) shall be divided. . . ."

Res gestae is an example of a Latin lawyerism that can obscure a dangerous gap in analysis. Translated, it means "things done." In the early 1800's, it was used to denote statements that were made as part of the transaction in issue (the "things done") and that were therefore admissible in evidence despite the hearsay rule. Perhaps because *res gestae* is far removed from ordinary English, lawyers and judges began to treat it as a ragbag. They used it carelessly to cover many different kinds of statements made at or about the time of the transaction in issue.[17] With policy and analysis obscured, *res gestae* became little more than a label to express the conclusion that a particular statement ought to be admitted into evidence over hearsay objection. Wigmore said: "The phrase 'res gestae' has long been not only entirely useless, but even positively harmful. . . . It is harmful, because by its ambiguity it invites the confusion of one

17. *See, e.g.,* cases described in Showalter v. Western Pacific R.R., 16 Cal.2d 460, 106 P.2d 895 (1940).

rule with another and thus creates uncertainty as to the limitations of both."[18]

The moral is this: Do not be too impressed by the Latin and archaic English words you read in law books. Their antiquity does not make them superior. When your pen is poised to write a lawyerism, stop to see if your meaning can be expressed as well or better in a word or two of ordinary English.

Exercise 7

Rewrite these sentences without the lawyerisms.

a. Said defendant International Business Machines Corp. is hereinafter referred to as "IBM."

b. The purpose of paragraph 9(f) is *in ambiguo,* but it appears to be mere *pro majori cautela.*

c. The patent laws which give a seventeen-year monopoly on "making, using, or selling the invention" are *in pari materia* with the antitrust laws and modify them *pro tanto.* That was the *ratio decidendi* of the *General Electric* case.

Compare your answers with those suggested on page 69. More exercises are on pages 75-76.

18. 6 J. WIGMORE, EVIDENCE § 1767 at 255 (Chadbourne rev. ed. 1976).

Chapter Four — Use Short Sentences

For several hundred years, English speaking lawyers have been addicted to long, complicated sentences. The long sentence habit began when English had no regular system of punctuation. But in law, the habit persisted long after orderly division of thought had become routine in ordinary English prose. When lawyers write, they deliver to the reader in one gigantic package all their main themes, supporting reasons, details, qualifications, exceptions, and conclusions. In particular, statutes and regulations wind on line after line, perhaps on the theory that if the readers come to a period they will rush out to violate the law without bothering to read on to the end. For example, here is section 631(a) of the California Penal Code:

> Any person who, by means of any machine, instrument, or contrivance, or in any manner, intentionally taps, or makes any unauthorized connection, whether physically, electrically, acoustically, inductively, or otherwise, with any telegraph or telephone wire, line, cable, or instrument of any internal telephonic communications system, or who willfully and without consent of all parties to the communication, or in any unauthorized manner, reads, or attempts to read, or to learn the contents or meaning of any message,

report, or communication while the same is in transit or passing over any such wire, line or cable, or is being sent from or received at any place within this state; or who uses, or attempts to use, in any manner, or for any purpose, or to communicate in any way, any information so obtained, or who aids, agrees with, employs, or conspires with any person or persons to unlawfully do, or permit, or cause to be done any of the acts or things mentioned above in this section, is punishable by a fine not exceeding two thousand five hundred dollars ($2,500), or by imprisonment in the county jail not exceeding one year, or by imprisonment in the state prison not exceeding three years, or by both such fine and imprisonment in the county jail or in the state prison.[19]

That sentence contains 242 words and no fewer than eighteen separate thoughts. Little wonder it is hard to swallow.[20]

A. *Short Sentences Aid Comprehension*

Long sentences make legal writing hard to understand. To prove this to yourself, read the following passage once at your normal speed. Then ask yourself what it means.

In a trial by jury, the court may, when the convenience of witnesses or the ends of justice would be promoted thereby, on motion of a party, after notice and hearing, make an order, no later than the close of the pretrial conference in cases in which such pretrial conference is to be held, or, in other cases, no later

19. CAL. PEN. CODE § 631(a) (West 1970).

20. The leading candidate for longest statutory passage, § 341(e)(1) of the Internal Revenue Code, contains 522 words.

than 10 days before the trial date, that the trial of the issue of liability shall precede the trial of any other issue in the case. . . .[21]

The subject matter of that passage is not profound or complicated, but the passage is hard to understand. It consists of a single sentence, eighty-six words long, containing five pieces of information. It tells us that:

(1) in a jury case, the liability issue may be tried before any other issue;

(2) the judge may order this if it will serve the convenience of witnesses or the ends of justice;

(3) the order may be made on a party's motion, after notice and hearing;

(4) in a case with a pretrial conference, the order must be made before the end of the conference; and

(5) in a case with no pretrial conference, the order must be made at least ten days before the trial date.

The passage is hard to understand for two reasons. First, the single sentence format caused the author to distort the logical order of the five pieces of information. The first thing the readers want to know is what the passage is about. It is about the trial of the liability issue before the other issues. But the readers do not discover that until they have climbed through a thicket of subsidiary ideas and arrived at the last twenty words of the sentence. Second, the single sentence format strains the readers' memories. The subject of the sentence *(court)* appears at word seven. At word thirty-two, the verb *(make)* finally shows up. Part of the object *(an order)*

21. CAL. CIV. PROC. CODE § 598 (West 1976) (amended 1977).

comes next, but the critical part remains hidden until the readers arrive, breathless, at word sixty-eight. By then they have forgotten the subject and verb and must search back in the sentence to find them.

The remedy for such a passage is simple. Instead of one long sentence containing five thoughts, use five sentences, each containing one thought. Here is one way the passage could be rewritten:

> In a jury case, the court may order the liability issue to be tried before any other issue. This may be done if the court finds that it would serve the convenience of witnesses or the ends of justice. The order may be made on the motion of a party, after notice and hearing. In cases where a pretrial conference is held, the order must be made before the end of the conference. In other cases the order must be made at least ten days before the trial date.

In place of one eighty-seven word sentence, we now have five sentences with an average length of eighteen words. Each sentence contains only one main thought, and the thoughts follow in logical sequence.

B. A Guide to Clarity

Passages like the one above suggest a two-part guide to clarity and ease of understanding in legal writing:

(1)   In most sentences, put only one main thought.

(2)   Keep the average sentence length below twenty-five words.

Do not misinterpret this guide. The first part says that *most* sentences should contain only one main thought. It does not say that *every* sentence should contain only one main thought. The second part says that the *average* length of your sentences should be below twenty-five words.[22] It does *not* say that every sentence should be twenty-five words or less. A succession of short, simple sentences sounds choppy:

> Defense counsel objected to the question. She argued that it called for hearsay. The court overruled the objection. The witness was allowed to answer.

You need an occasional longer sentence in which two or more main thoughts are joined:

> Defense counsel objected to the question, arguing that it called for hearsay; the court overruled the objection, and the witness was allowed to answer.

But when you write a long sentence, bear in mind Mark Twain's advice. After recommending short sentences as the general rule, he added:

22. To measure the length of your sentences, pick a sample passage and count the number of words from one period to the next. Count hyphenated words and groups of symbols as one word. Do not count citations. For example, this sentence would be counted as 20 words:

1	2	3	4	5	6	7	8

The twin-drive concept was obvious from IBM's '497 pat-

9	10	11	12	13		14	15

ent; under the *Graham* test, 382 U.S. at 17–18, that is

16	17	18	19	20

enough to invalidate Claim 12.

When you measure a tabulated sentence (see pages 39–40, *infra*), regard the initial colon and the semicolons as periods. *See*

At times [the writer] may indulge himself with a long
one, but he will make sure that there are no folds in it,
no vaguenesses, no parenthetical interruptions of its
view as a whole; when he has done with it, it won't be
a sea-serpent with half of its arches under the water; it
will be a torch-light procession.[23]

Exercise 8

*Rewrite these passages, using short sentences and omitting as many
surplus words as you can.*

   a. By establishing a technique whereby the claims of
      many individuals can be resolved at the same time,
      class actions serve an important function in our
      judicial system in eliminating the possibility of
      repetitious litigation and providing claimants with
      a method of obtaining enforcement of claims
      which would otherwise be too small to warrant
      individual litigation.

   b. While there are instances in which consumer abuse
      and exploitation result from advertising which is
      false, misleading, or irrelevant, it does not neces-
      sarily follow that these cases need to be remedied

---

generally T. BERNSTEIN, WATCH YOUR LANGUAGE 111–21
(Atheneum paperback ed. 1976); R. FLESCH, THE ART OF
PLAIN TALK 49–57 (Collier paperback ed. 1951); Fry, *A Read-
ability Formula That Saves Time,* 11 JOURNAL OF READING 513
(1968).

23. As quoted in E. GOWERS, THE COMPLETE PLAIN WORDS
183 (Fraser rev. ed. 1973).

by governmental intervention in the marketplace because it is possible for consumers' interests to be protected through resort to the courts, either by consumers themselves or by those competing sellers who see their market shares decline in the face of inroads based on such advertising.

Compare your answers with those suggested on page 69. More exercises are on pages 76-77.

C. Use Tabulation to Split Up Long Sentences

Sometimes the shortest, clearest way to present a complicated piece of material is in one long sentence, split up like a laundry list. This device is called tabulation. You will see one example on page 35, above. Here is another, a statement of the damage rules followed in contract interference cases:

One who is liable to another for interference with a contract or prospective advantageous economic relation is liable for damages for:

(a) the pecuniary loss of the benefits of the contract or the prospective relation;

(b) other pecuniary loss for which the interference is a legal cause; and

(c) emotional distress or actual harm to reputation, if they are reasonably to be expected to result from the interference.[24]

When you tabulate, follow these conventions:[25]

---

24. RESTATEMENT (SECOND) OF TORTS § 744A(1) (Tent. Draft No. 23, 1977).

25. *See* R. DICKERSON, THE FUNDAMENTALS OF LEGAL DRAFTING 85–86 (1965).

(1) The items in the list must be of the same class. (Don't make a list of (a) bread, (b) eggs, and (c) Czar Nicholas II.)

(2) The items in the list must fit, in substance and grammar, with the material in front of the colon. If the sentence continues past the last item in the list, the concluding material must fit also.

(3) The items in the list should be indented to set them apart from the material before and after.

(4) The items in the list should begin with a lower case letter.

(5) If the last item in the list is the end of the sentence, it should end with a period. If it is not the end of the sentence, it should end with a semicolon.

(6) The next-to-last item in the list should end with a semicolon followed by *or* (if the list is disjunctive) or *and* (if the list is conjunctive.)

(7) The other items in the list should end with semicolons.[26]

As the preceding paragraph shows, you can also use tabulation to bring order to a series of related, complete sentences. Use the preceding paragraph as a guide to the conventional form and punctuation of that type of tabulation.

26. When the items on the list are complicated you can put "; and" or "; or" after each item in the list except the last. That helps the reader stay on track. *See, e.g.*, the Federal Rules of Evidence.

Exercise 9

Rewrite this sentence in tabulated form.

You can qualify for benefits under section 43 if you are sixty-four or older and unable to work, and that section also provides benefits in the event that you are blind in one eye, or in both eyes, or are injured in the course of your employment.

Compare your answer with the one on page 69. More exercises are on pages 79-80.

Chapter Five—Use Base Verbs and the Active Voice

These two passages say the same thing. Which of them do you prefer?

> *Passage One:* The conclusion which has been reached by my client is that if there is a continuation of your insistence on this position, the termination of the contract will be taken into serious consideration by her.

> *Passage Two:* My client has concluded that if you continue to insist on this position, she will seriously consider terminating the contract.

Passage Two is better, is it not? Passage One clanks along like a rusty tank. It is an overblown example of two common legal writing faults: (1) the writer has overused the passive voice, and (2) the writer has converted crisp base verbs (like *continue*) into sodden derivative nouns (like *continuation*).

A. Base Verbs v. Derivative Nouns and Adjectives

At its core, the law is not abstract; it is part of a real world full of people who live and move and do things to other people. Car drivers *collide*. Plaintiffs *complain*. Judges *decide*. Defendants *pay*. To express this life and motion, a writer must use verbs—action words. The purest verb form is the base verb, like *collide, complain,*

decide, and *pay.* Base verbs are simple creatures. They
cannot tolerate adornment. If you try to dress them up,
you squash their life and motion. Unfortunately, that is
done all too easily. The base verb *collide* can be decked
out as a derivative noun, *collision.* Likewise, *complain*
becomes *complaint, decide* becomes *decision,* and *pay*
becomes *payment.* Lawyers love to ruin base verbs. Lawyers don't *act*—they *take action.* They don't *assume*—they
make assumptions. They don't *conclude*—they *draw conclusions.* With too much of this, legal writing becomes a
lifeless vapor.

When a base verb is replaced by a derivative noun or
adjective, surplus words begin to swarm like gnats.
"Please *state* why you *object* to the question," comes out
like this: "Please *make a statement* of why you *are inter-
posing an objection* to the question." The base verb *state*
can do the work all alone. But to get the same work out
of *statement,* you need a supporting verb *(make),* an article
(a), and a preposition *(of).* The derivative noun *objection*
attracts a similar cloud of surplus words.

Do not conclude from this that derivative nouns and
adjectives are always bad; sometimes you need them. But
do not overuse them in place of base verbs. You can spot
the common ones by their endings: *-ment, -ion, -ance,
-ence, -ancy, -ency, -ant,* and *-ent.* When you spot one, stop
to see if you can make your sentence stronger and
shorter by using a base verb instead.

Exercise 10

*Rewrite these sentences, omitting surplus words and using
base verbs in place of derivative nouns and adjectives.*

a. Section 1038 has pertinence to any contract which makes provision for attorney fees.

b. Commencement of discovery is not dependent on the judge's consideration of the motion.

c. We are in agreement with your argument, but if it is your intention to cause delay, we will stand in opposition to you.

d. The effectuation of improvement in downstream water quality has as a requirement our termination of the pollution of the headwaters.

Compare your answers with those suggested on page 70. More exercises are on pages 80-81.

B. The Active Voice v. The Passive Voice

When you use the active voice, the subject of the sentence acts: "The union filed a complaint." When you use the passive voice, the subject of the sentence is acted upon: "A complaint was filed by the union."

The passive voice has two disadvantages. First, it takes more words. When you say, "the union filed a complaint," *filed* does the work by itself. But when you say, "a complaint was filed by the union," the verb *filed* requires a supporting verb *(was)* and a preposition *(by)*. Here are other examples:

Passive Voice	*Active Voice*
the ruling was made by the trial judge that	the trial judge ruled that
our interpretation is supported by the legislative history	the legislative history supports our interpretation
the trust was intended by the trustor to	the trustor intended the trust to

The second disadvantage of the passive voice is its detached abstraction. With the active voice, the reader can usually see who is doing what to whom. But the passive voice often leaves that unclear:

> It is feared that adequate steps will not be taken to mitigate the damages which are being caused.

Who is doing the fearing? Who is supposed to take the steps? Who is causing the damages? We cannot tell because the actor in each case is hidden in the fog of the passive voice.

The passive voice can be particularly noxious in technical legal writing. Consider this patent license provision:

> All improvements of the patented invention which are made hereafter shall promptly be disclosed, and failure to do so shall be deemed a material breach of this license agreement.

Who must disclose what to whom? Must the licensee disclose improvements it makes to the licensor? Must the licensor disclose improvements it makes to the licensee? Must each party disclose the improvements it makes to the other party? If it ever becomes important, the parties probably will have to fight it out in an expensive lawsuit.

The passive voice has its proper uses. First, you can use it when the thing done is important, and the one who did it is not:

> The summons and complaint were served on January 19th.

Second, you can use it where the actor is unknown or indefinite:

> The ledgers were mysteriously destroyed.

Third, you can use it to place a strong element at the end of the sentence for emphasis:

In the defendant's closet was found the bloody coat.

Fourth, you can use it on those rare occasions when detached abstraction is appropriate:

All people were created with a thirst for knowledge.

But elsewhere, use the active voice; it will make your writing stronger, briefer, and clearer.

Exercise 11

Rewrite these sentences using the active voice and omitting surplus words.

a. Clients' funds which have been received by an attorney must be put into the Client Trust Account.

b. This agreement may be terminated by either party by thirty days' notice being given to the other.

c. Each month price lists were exchanged between the defendant manufacturers, and it was agreed by them that all sales would be made at list price or above.

d. If I am not survived by my husband by thirty days, my children are to receive hereunder such of those items of my personal property as may be selected by my executor for them.

Compare your answers with those suggested on page 70. More exercises are on page 81.

Chapter Six—Arrange Your Words With Care

In some languages, the order of words within a sentence does not affect the sentence meaning. But in English, word order does affect meaning, as this sentence shows:

> The defendant was arrested for fornicating under a little-used state statute.

To avoid that sort of gaffe, you must take care in arranging your words.

A. Normal Word Order and Inversion for Emphasis

To make your writing easy to understand, most of your sentences should follow the normal English word order—first the subject, then the verb, and then the object (if there is one):

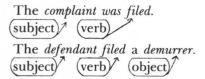

The *complaint was filed.*
(subject) (verb)
The *defendant filed* a *demurrer.*
(subject) (verb) (object)

If you want to emphasize a word, the strongest place to put it is at the end of the sentence. The next-strongest place is at the beginning of the sentence. Suppose that in this sentence you want to emphasize the word *conspiracy:*

> Plaintiff's complaint makes a conspiracy charge against the defendants.

One way is to put *conspiracy* at the beginning of the sentence:

> Conspiracy is charged in plaintiff's complaint against defendants.

But the emphasis is stronger if you put *conspiracy* at the end of the sentence:

> Plaintiff's complaint charges the defendants with conspiracy.

Note that in each of the three sentences the subject comes before the verb. On rare occasion, you may want to place extra stress on the subject by inverting the normal word order and putting the subject at the end of the sentence:

> Basic to our liberties is fair procedure.

Exercise 12

Rewrite these sentences to emphasize the words right to counsel.

   a. The defendant's right to counsel is guaranteed by the sixth amendment.
   b. The defendant is denied the right to counsel if the defendant's lawyer is barred from speaking.

Rewrite this sentence, inverting the normal word order to emphasize the words the stench of perjury.

   c. The stench of perjury lingers in every word the witness spoke.

Compare your answers with those suggested on page 70. More exercises are on pages 81-82.

B. Keep the Subject Close to the Verb and the Verb Close to the Object

Lawyers like to test the agility of their readers by making them leap wide gaps between the subject and the verb and between the verb and the object. For example:

> A claim, which in the case of negligent misconduct shall not exceed $500, and in the case of intentional misconduct shall not exceed $1,000, may be filed with the Office of the Administrator by any injured party.

In that sentence the reader must span a twenty-two word crevasse to get from the subject *(claim)* to the verb *(may be filed)*. The best remedy for a gap this wide is to turn the intervening words into a separate sentence:

> Any injured party may file a clam with the Office of Administrator. A claim shall not exceed $500 for negligent misconduct, nor $1,000 for intentional misconduct.

Smaller gaps between subject and verb can be closed by moving the intervening words to the beginning or end of the sentence:

Gap	*Gap Closed*
This agreement, unless revocation has occurred at an earlier date, shall expire on November 1, 1989.	Unless sooner revoked, this agreement shall expire on November 1, 1989.
The defendant, in addition to having to pay punitive damages, may be liable for plaintiff's costs and attorney fees.	The defendant may have to pay plaintiff's costs and attorney fees, in addition to punitive damages.

The problem is the same when the gap comes between the verb and the object:

The proposed statute gives to any person who suffers financial injury by reason of discrimination based on race, religion, sex, or physical handicap a cause of action for treble damages.

Here a twenty-one word gap comes between the verb *(gives)* and the direct object *(cause of action)*. One remedy is to make two sentences. Another is to move the intervening words to the end of the sentence:

The proposed statute gives a cause of action for treble damages to any person who suffers financial injury by reason of discrimination based on race, religion, sex, or physical handicap.

Exercise 13

Close the gaps in these sentences by moving the intervening words or by splitting the sentence into two. When you rewrite, omit surplus words.

a. A response must, within twenty days after service of the petition has been made, be filed with the hearing officer.

b. The attorney-client privilege, while applying to the client's revelation of a past crime, has no application when the client seeks the aid of the attorney to make plans for the commission of a future crime.

c. The sole eyewitness, having seen the accident from the window of an apartment which was on the seventh floor of a building located one-half block in a northerly direction from the intersection, testified that she did not see which car made the first entry into the intersection.

d. Jose Cruz, who was the plaintiff's grandfather, later transferred, by a deed of gift which was bitterly contested by the heirs but which was ultimately upheld by the probate court, the 200 acres which are in dispute.

Compare your answers with those suggested on pages 70-71. More exercises are on page 82.

C. Put Modifying Words Close to What They Modify

Modifying words tend to do their work on whatever you put them near. For example, this sentence conveys three different pictures, depending on where you put the modifier:

The judge ordered the marshal to eject the photographer. who was kicking and screaming.

As a general rule, put modifying words as close as you can to what you want them to modify. That will help avoid sentences like these:

My client has discussed your proposal to fill the drainage ditch with his partners.

The defendant is accused of assaulting Professor Appleman while he was teaching a class maliciously and with intent to do great bodily harm.

Being beyond any doubt insane, Judge Weldon ordered the petitioner's transfer to a state mental hospital.

Beware of the "squinting" modifier—one which sits mid-sentence and can be read to modify either what precedes it or what follows it:

A trustee who steals dividends often cannot be punished.

What does *often* modify? Does the sentence tell us that crime frequently pays? Or that frequent crime pays?

Squinting modifiers are especially mischievous in technical legal instruments:

> If this contract is terminated under paragraph 3(d)(1), Agent shall be notified immediately to cancel all outstanding workorders.

What must be immediate, the notice or the cancellation?

Once discovered, a squinting modifier is easily cured. Either choose a word that does not squint, or rearrange the sentence to avoid the ambiguity. In the last example, *immediately* could be put before *notified* or after *cancel,* whichever would express the parties' intent.[27]

The word *only* is a notorious troublemaker in legal writing. For example, in this sentence, the word *only* could go in any of seven places and produce a half a dozen different meanings:

> She said that he shot her.

To keep *only* under control, put it immediately before the word you want it to modify. If it creates ambiguity in that position, try to isolate it at the beginning or the end of the sentence:

Ambiguous	*Clear*
Lessee shall use the vessel only for recreation.	Lessee shall use the vessel for recreation only.
Shares are sold to the public only by the parent corporation.	Only the parent corporation sells shares to the public.

27. You might also put *immediately* between *to* and *cancel,* but that would needlessly distract readers who believe that infinitives should not be split. Those same readers will be distracted if you end a sentence with a preposition when you do not need to.

Watch out for ambiguity in sentences like this one:

> The grantor was Maxwell Aaron, the father of Sarah Aaron, who later married Pat Snyder.

Who married Pat—Maxwell or Sarah? Some lawyers try to clear up such ambiguity by piling on more words:

> The grantor was Maxwell Aaron, father of Sarah Aaron, which said Maxwell Aaron latter married Pat Snyder.

But it's easier than that. You can usually avoid ambiguity by placing the relative pronoun (like *who, which,* and *that*) right after the word to which it relates. If Pat's spouse were Maxwell, the sentence could be rearranged to read:

> The grantor was Sarah Aaron's father, Maxwell Aaron, who later married Pat Snyder.

Sometimes a relative pronoun will not behave, no matter where you put it:

> Claims for expenses, which must not exceed $100, must be made within 30 days.

What must not exceed $100—the claims or the expenses? Here the best remedy is simply to cut out the relative pronoun:

> Claims for expenses must not exceed $100 and must be made within 30 days.

> or

> Expenses must not exceed $100. Claims for expenses must be made within 30 days.

Exercise 14

Rewrite these sentences to solve the modifier problems. If a sentence has more than one possible meaning, select whichever one you wish and rewrite the sentence to express that meaning without ambiguity.

a. When a worker is injured often no compensation is paid.

b. The plaintiff's pain can be alleviated only by expensive therapy.

c. Being ignorant of the law, the attorney argued that his client should receive a light sentence.

d. Defendant's argument overlooks an amendment to the statute which was enacted in 1971.

e. Under section 309, attorney fees only can be awarded when the claim is brought without good faith.

f. Apparently the capital gains provision was intended to encourage the production of cotton in the eyes of Congress.

Compare your answers with those suggested on page 71. More exercises are on pages 82-83.

Chapter Seven — Avoid Language Quirks

Language quirks are small distractions that draw your reader's mind from what you are saying to how you are saying it. Most of what lawyers write is read by people, not because they want to, but because they have to. Their attention is, therefore, prone to wander. Further, they are usually surrounded by outside distractions—the ring of the telephone, the cough at the library table, and the clock that tells them time is short. Language quirks add to those distractions and are thus to be avoided.

A. Elegant Variation

Elegant variation[28] is practiced by writers whose English teachers told them not to use the same word twice in one sentence. The practice produces sentences like this:

> The first case was settled for $2,000, and the second piece of litigation was disposed of out of court for $3,000, while the price of the amicable accord reached in the third suit was $5,000.

28. H. Fowler, A Dictionary of Modern English Usage 148–51 (2d ed. E. Gowers 1965).

The readers are left to ponder the difference between a *case,* a *piece of litigation,* and a *suit.* By the time they conclude that there is no difference, they have no patience left for *settled, disposed of out of court,* and *amicable accord,* much less for what the writer was trying to tell them in the first place.

Elegant variation is particularly vexing in technical legal writing. The reader of a formal instrument is entitled to assume that a shift in terms is intended to signal a shift in meaning, and the reader is justifiably puzzled at passages like this:

> The use fee shall be 1% of Franchisee's gross revenue. Franchise payments shall be made on or before the 15th day of each month.

Are *franchise payments* something different than the *use fee?* If so, what are they, and when must the use fee be paid?

Do not be afraid to repeat a word if it is the right word and if repeating it will avoid confusion. If the repetition sounds clumsy, try a pronoun or recast the sentence:

The arresting officers did not inform the defendant of her right to remain silent, and the arresting officers did not permit the defendant to call her lawyer.	The arresting officers did not inform the defendant of her right to remain silent, and they did not permit her to call her lawyer.
The plaintiff alleges that he was deprived of his rights under the first amendment and under the fourteenth amendment.	The plaintiff alleges that he was deprived of his rights under the first and fourteenth amendments.

Only slightly less confusing than elegant variation is the use of a word in one sense and its repetition shortly after in a different sense:

> The majority opinion gives no consideration to appellant's argument that no consideration was given for the promise.

The remedy is obvious—replace one of the pair with a different term:

> The majority opinion ignores appellant's argument that no consideration was given for the promise.

B. Noun Chain Confusion Avoidance Technique

As the heading of this section demonstrates, a long chain of nouns used as adjectives is apt to strangle the reader. Military writers are fond of noun chains. They have their *radiation contamination detection devices,* their *retrograde motion simulation capabilities,* and their *programmed precounterinsurgency countermeasures.* Lawyers are not immune. They have been known to make *cease and desist order compliance investigation reports* and to file *pretrial document identification requests.*

To bring a noun chain under control, lop off any of the descriptive words that are unnecessary. If that is not enough, then insert some words to break up the chain, like this: "request for pretrial identification of documents."

C. Sexism in Legal Writing

The time has passed when legal writers can pretend that the world is inhabited by males only. Women are tired of being told that "words importing the masculine gender include the feminine as well."[29] But writing gen-

29. 1 U.S.C. § 1(1970).

derless English is not easy. If you write "each judge has his own ideals," you will be faulted for ignoring the women on the bench. If you write "each judge has his or her own ideals," you will be faulted for clumsy construction. If you write "all judges have their own ideals," you will be faulted for not stating clearly what you mean.

Nonetheless, the sex bias of our language can be mitigated in several ways:

(1) Avoid expressions that imply value judgments based on sex:

> a man-size job
>
> a manly effort
>
> took it like a man
>
> a real sob sister
>
> an old-maid attitude
>
> a member of the weaker sex

(2) Avoid expressions that suggest that men are the only people on earth:

Avoid	Use
man's basic liberties	basic human liberties
reasonable man	reasonable person
the wisdom of man	human wisdom

(3) Avoid sex based descriptions and titles when there are reasonable substitutes:

Avoid	Use
workman	worker
congressmen	members of Congress
policeman	police officer
mayoress	mayor
authoress	author

foreman	supervisor
newsman	journalist

(4) When referring to both sexes, use parallel construction:

Avoid	*Use*
men and their wives	husbands and wives
ladies and men	men and women, ladies and gentlemen
President Washington and Martha	President and Mrs. Washington

(5) Avoid using masculine singular pronouns when the referent is not necessarily male. Phrases like *he or she* can be used in moderation, but it is usually less clumsy to recast the sentence in one of these ways:

(a) Omit the pronoun:

The average citizen enjoys his time on the jury.	The average citizen enjoys jury duty.

(b) Use the second person in place of the third person:

Each juror must think for himself.	As a juror, you must think for yourself.

(c) Use the plural in place of the singular:

Each juror believes that he has done something worthwhile.	All jurors believe that they have done something worthwhile.

(d) If you are desperate, you can recast the sentence in the passive voice, but that has its own drawbacks.[30]

30. *See* page 45–47, *supra.*

D. Adjective-Adverb Mania

Most legal writing is declaratory. It simply states the facts, without comment and without trying to persuade anyone of anything. Statutes, apartment leases, corporate bylaws, and bills of lading fall in this category. But some legal writing does comment; through commentary, it seeks to persuade the reader to believe what the writer believes. Legal briefs and judicial opinions are obvious examples. Where commentary is appropriate, it will be more potent if you use strong nouns and verbs, not weak nouns and verbs held afloat by adjectives and adverbs:

Adjectives and Adverbs	*Nouns and Verbs*
The witness intentionally testified untruthfully about the cargo.	The witness lied about the cargo.
Defendant's sales agents maliciously took advantage of people with little money and limited intelligence.	Defendant's sales agents preyed on the poor and ignorant.

When you need to use an adjective or adverb for commentary, choose one that fits. Do not use a fiery one and then douse it with water:

> rather catastrophic
>
> somewhat terrified
>
> a bit malevolently
>
> slightly hysterical

Likewise, do not choose a flaccid one and then try to prop it up with words like *very, much,* and *quite:*

Weak	*Strong*
she was very, very angry	she was enraged
this is quite puzzling	this is baffling
there was much confusion in the courtroom	the courtroom was chaotic

Adjective-adverb mania sometimes produces terms like "real facts." Are there any "unreal facts"? If a witness is described as telling the "honest truth," what are we to say of those who tell only the "truth"? Is a "dead murder victim" any colder than a "murder victim"? Is a "completely revoked" contract offer any more lifeless than one that has only been "revoked"? What are we to say when asked our "actual age"? To avoid all this, forget the adjectives and adverbs and let the nouns and verbs do their work.

E. Throat-Clearing

Just as some public speakers clear their throats at every pause, some legal writers feel the need to clear the clogs from their pens every fifty words or so. The result is a collection of phrases like this:

> It is important to add that. . . .
>
> Clear beyond dispute is the fact that. . . .
>
> It may be recalled that. . . .
>
> In this regard it is of significance that. . . .
>
> It is interesting to point out that. . . .

William Zinsser writes:

> If you might add, add it. If it should be pointed out, point it out. If it is interesting to note, *make* it inter-

esting. Being told that something is interesting is the surest way of tempting the reader to find it dull. . . .[31]

Words like *clearly* are favorite throat clearers. California's former Chief Justice Roger Traynor used to tell his law clerks to strike *clearly* whenever they used it: if what is said is clear, then *clearly* is not needed, and if it is not clear, then *clearly* will not make it so.

Exercise 15

Rewrite this paragraph to rid it of language quirks.

It goes without saying that every attorney has a mandatory ethical duty to protect what he learns in confidence about his clients. Clearly, this ethical requirement covers what the client tells his lawyer in confidence. But of equal importance, this duty imposed by the rules of ethics covers what third parties relate to the practitioner of law about his client, if the client has asked that such material be kept secret, or if revealing the third-party-derived, client-related information would harm or embarrass the client.

Compare your answer with the one on page 71. More exercises are on page 83.

---

31. W. Zinsser, On Writing Well 16 (1976).

Chapter Eight—Conclusion

You have now learned six principles of plain English:

1. Omit surplus words.

2. Use familiar, concrete words.

3. Use short sentences.

4. Use base verbs and the active voice.

5. Arrange your words with care.

6. Avoid language quirks.

To master these principles takes practice. That is why the exercises are included in this book. If you have ignored them up to now, go back and work them.

Remember, too, that a lawyer who writes plain English may not be loved by other lawyers. Economist John Kenneth Galbraith addressed this point when speaking of the need for plain English in his field. What he says applies equally to the law:

> [T]here are no important propositions that cannot be stated in plain language. . . . The writer who seeks to be intelligible needs to be right; he must be challenged if his argument leads to an erroneous conclusion and especially if it leads to the wrong action. But he can safely dismiss the charge that he has made the subject too easy. The truth is not difficult. Complexity and obscurity have professional value—they are the aca-

demic equivalents of apprenticeship rules in the building trades. They exclude the outsiders, keep down the
competition, preserve the image of a privileged or
priestly class. The man who makes things clear is a
scab. He is criticized less for his clarity than for his
treachery.[32]

32. Galbraith, *Writing, Typing & Economics*, ATLANTIC,
March 1978, at 105.

EXERCISE KEY

These are not "the answers" to the exercises. They are some of the many possible answers. You may often find that your answer is better than the one given here. That should be cause for cheer, not puzzlement.

1. With the working words circled, the original sentence looks like this:

In the event that there is a waiver of the attorney-client privilege by the client, the letters must be produced by the attorney for the purpose of inspection by the adversary party.

The original could be revised to read:

If the client waives the attorney-client privilege, the attorney must produce the letters for inspection by the adversary party.

With the working words circled, the revision looks like this:

If the client waives the attorney-client privilege, the attorney must produce the letters for inspection by the adversary party.

2. a. If the tenant defaults, the lease will terminate.

  b. For simplicity, an ordinary deed of trust would be the best.

  c. Before the enactment of the statute, the clause was added because the *Burke* decision seemed to require it.

  d. Plaintiff's brief contains several misstatements about the disputed time sequence.

  e. When the funds are received, we will transfer title to clear up all questions about this matter.

  f. Now the witness cannot recall what the letter was about.

3. a. When the judgment is entered. . . .

  b. Here estoppel can be invoked. . . .

    c. He was sentenced for five months. . . .

    d. By the terms of our contract. . . .

    e. No doubt the statute applies where. . . .

    f. The claim was clarified by a bill of particulars. . . .

    g. The trial judge must consider whether. . . .

    h. This offer will stand until you. . . .

    i. Under section 103(b), you are entitled. . . .

    j. Usually good faith is not disputed. . . .

    k. The plaintiff filed suit even though she knew that. . . .

    l. Arbitration is sometimes useful where the parties. . . .

    m. This point has troubled many courts. . . .

    n. Because he was injured. . . .

    o. Whether there was negligence. . . .

4. a. Appellant's opening brief contains three misstatements of fact.

    b. The lower court decree does not affect the stockholder's claim.

    c. The witness need not sign the deposition transcript until the reporter's errors are corrected.

    d. In approving a class action settlement, the court must guard the interests of absent class members.

    e. We cannot tell whether counsel's misconduct influenced the jury's verdict.

    f. The partition agreement between Smith and Hagen was superseded by the later court decree.

5. We turn now to plaintiff's request for an injunction. The defendant argues that an injunction is unnecessary, because the exclusionary clause is already void under this court's prior order. Since the exclusionary clause can have no further effect, the defendant argues that we can give the plaintiff relief without issuing an injunction. We agree.

6. a. The sky is falling.

b. One thing the Parole Board must consider is the prisoner's ability to get used to freedom.

c. Prison reform depends partly on how much the public knows about what is happening in prisons.

7. a. The defendant International Business Machines Corp. is here called "IBM."

   or simpler

   Defendant International Business Machines Corp. (IBM). . . .

   b. The purpose of paragraph 9(f) is unclear, but it seems to have been included only as an extra precaution.

   c. The patent laws, which give a seventeen-year monopoly on "making, using, or selling the invention," concern the same general subject as the antitrust laws, and the two should be construed together. The patent laws modify the antitrust laws to some extent. That is why *General Electric* was decided as it was.

8. a. Class actions serve an important function in our judicial system. They permit claims of many individuals to be resolved at the same time. This avoids repetitious litigation and gives claimants a way to enforce claims that are too small for individual litigation.

   b. Consumers are sometimes abused and exploited by false, misleading, or irrelevant advertising. But that does not necessarily require the government to intrude into the marketplace. Consumers themselves can go to court, as can competing sellers who lose business because of such advertising.

9. You can qualify for benefits under section 43 if you are:

   (a) sixty-four or older and unable to work;
   (b) blind in one or both eyes; or
   (c) injured in the course of your employment.

10. a. Section 1038 pertains to any contract which provides for attorney fees.

  b. Discovery can commence before the judge considers the motion.

  c. We agree with your argument, but if you intend to cause delay, we will oppose you.

  d. To improve downstream water quality, we must stop polluting the headwaters.

11. a. An attorney who receives clients' funds must put them in the Client Trust Account.

  b. Either party may terminate this agreement by giving thirty day's notice to the other.

  c. Each month the defendant manufacturers exchanged price lists, and they agreed to make all sales at list price or above.

  d. If my husband does not survive me by thirty days, I give my children such items of my personal property as my executor may select for them.

12. a. The sixth amendment guarantees the defendant's right to counsel.

  b. If the defendant's lawyer is barred from speaking, the defendant is denied the right to counsel.

  c. In every word the witness spoke lingers the stench of perjury.

13. a. A response must be filed with the hearing officer within twenty days after the petition is served.

  b. The attorney-client privilege applies to the client's revelation of a past crime. But it does not apply where the client seeks the attorney's aid to plan a future crime.

  c. The sole eyewitness saw the accident from a seventh floor apartment window, half a block north of the intersection. She testified that she did not see which car entered the intersection first.

  d. Plaintiff's grandfather, Jose Cruz, later transferred the disputed 200 acres by a deed of gift which was bitterly contested by the heirs but which was ultimately upheld by the probate court.

14   a. Often when a worker is injured, no compensation is paid.

    b. Only expensive therapy can alleviate plaintiff's pain.

    c. The attorney argued that his client, being ignorant of the law, should receive a light sentence.

    d. Defendant's argument overlooks a 1971 amendment to the statute.

    e. Only when the claim is brought without good faith can attorney fees be awarded under section 309.

    f. The capital gains provision was apparently intended, in the eyes of Congress, to encourage the production of cotton.

15. Attorneys have an ethical duty to protect what they learn in confidence from their clients. This ethical duty covers what the client tells the attorney in confidence. It also covers what third parties tell the attorney about the client if the client has asked that the information be kept secret, or if its disclosure would harm or embarrass the client.

MORE PRACTICE EXERCISES

CHAPTER TWO, PART A (Page 7) *How to Spot Bad Construction*

Circle the working words in the sentences below. Compare their number with the number of glue words. Then rewrite the sentences, circle the working words, and compare the result with the original.

1. We believe that the conclusion that emerges in the light of this history is that every presumption should be on the side of the preservation of rights granted by the common law, assuming that there is an absence of contrary indications in compelling statutory language or in the form of compelling social policy.

2. The language of the contract, and in addition the language that is used in the statute, is such that it appears to have been contemplated that there would be a regular contract, capable of enforcement, between independent parties who were dealing with each other at arm's length.

3. It is the fact that heroin totaling one hundred grams and cocaine totaling fifty grams were discovered by the agents at the time of the arrest of the appellant, but this fact standing alone fails to compel the conclusion that there was probable cause for the agents to believe that appellant's van had been used for the transportation of the drugs so discovered.

CHAPTER TWO, PART B (Page 10) *Avoid Compound Prepositions*

Rewrite these sentences without the compound constructions.

1. In connection with the plaintiff's damage claim, the testimony of Dr. Weiner was offered with a view to proving pain and suffering.

2. In order to prevail, Kirkpatrick must make a strong showing in terms of abuse of discretion insofar as the trial court's ruling in connection with severance is concerned.

3. As to the design of said product, provide the dates when tests were conducted, either prior to or subsequent to said accident, for the purpose of obtaining data in relation to fatigue points.

4. Because of the reason that the Klamath Indian treaty does not contain any similar provisions in respect of this subject, appellants argue that there is no basis for limiting any rights with regard to fishing on reservation lands held by virtue of the treaty.

5. In accordance with plaintiff's theory as respects foreseeability, Pastore's cries for the purpose of getting help could reasonably have been expected to call forth plaintiff's efforts with reference to rescuing Pastore in the event that the ladder slipped further by reason of the ice on the deck.

CHAPTER TWO, PART C (Page 12) *Trim Out Verbose Word Clusters*

Rewrite these sentences without the verbose word clusters.

1. At that point in time, the deputies were not conducting a "search," even though it is the fact that they were looking through the car windows.

2. This is an instance in which Federal Rule of Evidence 803(8) would allow the admission of public records, insofar as they are relevant.

3. It certainly is not the case that every union political activity can escape scrutiny simply because of the fact that the First Amendment protects free speech.

4. It is of equal importance in this instance that the employees should not be able to secure the benefits of the contract for the period of the strike, until such time as they are willing also to accept the burdens thereof.

5. There is no doubt but that the inspector was justified by the obvious nervousness of the skipper in this case in demanding that the cargo hold be opened for further examination of its contents in an effort to answer the question as to whether there was contraband aboard.

CHAPTER TWO, PART D (Page 14) *How to Shorten Clauses and Phrases*

Cut the surplus words from these sentences by shortening clauses and phrases.

1. The first contention which is made by Scholtz is that there was error in the determination which was made by the trial judge that the escrow agreement was not enforceable.

2. There are three compelling reasons to reject the argument that has been made by the petitioner to the effect that trademarks are not subject to cancellation in proceedings which have been initiated by the Federal Trade Commission.

3. Identify all communications, whether they are in the form of writing or whether they are oral, that you had, or that you claim to have had, with the defendant from and after June 27, 1979, through and including the present, on the subject of the alleged accident that is described in paragraphs 3 through 9 of plaintiff's complaint herein.

4. During the period that preceded the filing of this environmental protection suit, the interpretation of the variance clause was a matter of some doubt, but after the decision that was rendered in *Louisiana-Pacific,* there is no longer any ground for speculation about the inter-

pretation of that clause from the point of view of the EPA.

CHAPTER TWO, PART E (Page 17) Do Not Use Redundant Legal Phrases

Rewrite these sentences without the redundant legal phrases.

1. Upon the preliminary proofs submitted, the court orders and decrees that custody of said child be awarded to T unless and until there is a submission of clear, substantial, and convincing evidence that R is a fitting and proper parent.

2. Accordingly, my client hereby gives notice under and in pursuance of paragraph 9(f), that the contract be and hereby is terminated from and after this date, and that said contract is of no further force or effect whatsover.

3. It is my desire and intention to give and provide to my beloved step-daughter, Angelina, a full, complete, and adequate education, and for that purpose and use, I do hereby give, devise, and bequeath unto her, to have and to hold, all my right, title, and interest in and to the properties described hereinbelow.

4. By virtue of the aforementioned instrument, which was duly executed and sworn under oath, the grantor authorized and empowered the agent to act with the same force and effect as she herself might have acted, save and except with respect to trust property.

CHAPTER THREE, PARTS A & B (Pages 25 & 27) Use Familiar, Concrete Words

Rewrite these sentences using familiar, concrete words.

1. Implementation of the foregoing regulations will be deferred pending the effectuation of approval thereof by the AMLB.

2. Increased mutual interreactions between parole officers and parolees not infrequently results in actualization of optimal conditions for restoration of parolees' employment status in positions held prior to confinement.

3. The conclusion we have reached is that the effectuation of beneficial changes in the relational atmosphere between the judges and the clerks will be dependent, in significant part, upon augmentation of the sense of responsibility felt or perceived by the clerks as such. That is to say, the clerks as a group should be made to understand and appreciate more fully than is now the case that the work they do is an integral and vital component of the internal functioning of the court itself. Further, negative reinforcement in the form of criticism should be minimized to the extent possible, and positive feedback and evaluation of clerks' work-product should be forthcoming whenever feasible and warranted by the circumstances.

CHAPTER THREE, PART C (Page 28) *Do Not Use Lawyerisms*

Rewrite these sentences without the lawyerisms.

1. The within Agreement and License constitutes the entire understanding and agreement between the parties hereto with respect to the subject matter hereof, and no modification or amendment hereof shall be valid or binding upon the parties hereto unless said modification or amendment is made in writing and signed on behalf of each of the parties by their respective proper officers thereunto duly authorized.

2. Judgment upon any arbitration award which may be rendered as hereinabove provided may be entered in any court having jurisdiction thereof, or application may be made by either of the parties hereto to such court for judicial acceptance of said award and for an order of enforcement, as the case may be.

3. NOW THEREFORE, BE IT KNOWN that in consider-

ation of the premises as well as in consideration of the sum of Five Thousand Dollars ($5,000) paid in hand by Licensor to Licensee contemporaneously with the delivery by Licensor to Licensee of a duly executed copy of this Agreement, and the royalty payments herein specified as well as in consideration of the terms, conditions, and covenants herein set forth, it is mutually agreed and covenanted by and between Licensor and Licensee as follows. . . .

4. We are inclined to a different view, *viz.*, that defendant, having been detected *in flagrante delicto,* can hardly be heard to complain that *causa proxima non remota spectatur.*

CHAPTER FOUR, PART B (Page 36) *Use Short Sentences*

Rewrite these passages using short sentences.

1. Notwithstanding a provision of irrevocability in the lawyer's contract of employment, the client has the power to discharge the lawyer at any time for any reason, and this is true even where the lawyer is said to have a "power coupled with an interest" or where the lawyer's fee is contingent, because the relationship of lawyer and client calls for continuing confidence, and if the confidence ends, the relationship should end.

2. The generalization that criminality is closely associated with poverty does not apply to white-collar criminals, for it has been observed that with few exceptions they are not from poor backgrounds, nor were they reared in slums, nor did they come from broken families, and they are usually neither feebleminded nor psychopathic. While conventional criminologists are fond of stating that "the criminal of today was the problem child of yesterday," white-collar criminals were seldom problem children who appeared in juvenile courts or child-guidance clinics, thus casting serious doubt on the notion that the causes of all kinds of criminality are to be found exclusively in childhood.

3. When a decedent leaves no real property, nor interest therein nor lien thereon, in this State, and the total value

of the decedent's property in this State, over and above any amounts due to the decedent for services in the armed forces of the United States, does not exceed one thousand dollars ($1,000), the surviving spouse, the children, lawful issue of deceased children, the parent, the brother or sister of the decedent, or the guardian of the estate of any minor or insane or incompetent person bearing such relationship to the decedent, if such person has a right to succeed to the property of the decedent, or is the sole beneficiary under the last will and testament of the decedent, may, without procuring letters of administration, or awaiting the probate of the will, collect any money due the decedent, receive the property of the decedent, and have any evidence of interest, indebtedness or right transferred to him upon furnishing the person, representative, corporation, officer or body owing the money, having custody of such property or acting as registrar or transfer agent of such evidences of interest, indebtedness or right, with an affadavit showing the right of the affiant or affiants to receive such money or property or to have such evidences transferred.

CHAPTER FOUR, PART C (Page 39) *Tabulation*

Rewrite these passages using tabulation.

1. My client is willing to settle this case for $7,500, to be paid by your client, and your client must immediately return the blueprints and specifications and must remove all of its equipment from the property. Moreover, my client insists upon having replacement of the entire section of fence which your client took down, the replacement to be at your client's expense.

2. The issuance of an injunction is not proper in order to stay proceedings in a court of the United States, and likewise injunctive relief is not available to stay proceedings in another state upon a judgment of a court of that state. By the same token, an injunction will not issue to prevent the execution of a public statute by officers of the law for the public benefit, nor to prevent the breach

of a contract, other than certain personal service contracts, the performance of which would not be specifically enforced, nor to prevent the exercise of a public or private office, in a lawful manner, by the person in possession.

3. Every person who unlawfully throws out a switch, removes a rail, or places any obstruction on any railroad with the intention of derailing any passenger, freight or other train, car or engine and thus derails the same, or who unlawfully places any dynamite or other explosive material or any other obstruction upon or near the track of any railroad with the intention of blowing up or derailing any such train, car or engine and thus blows up or derails the same, or who unlawfully sets fire to any railroad bridge or tressle over which any such train, car or engine must pass with the intention of wrecking such train, car or engine, and thus wrecks the same, is guilty of a felony.

CHAPTER FIVE, PART A (Page 43) *Use Base Verbs*

Rewrite these sentences using base verbs in place of the derivative nouns and adjectives.

1. Plaintiffs make an objection to paragraph 9 of the Proposed Pretrial Order on the ground that Defendants have provided no definition of the term "unsanitary."

2. Amendment of the complaint is one of our possible courses of action, but if we make a substitution of parties at this late date, we may find the court hesitant to place reliance on our estoppel argument.

3. The testator's intendment was given imperfect expression in the will, but it is our contention that fulfillment of the testator's wishes is impossible of accomplishment without termination of the *inter vivos* trust.

4. Our committee has given careful consideration to the fact that many lawyers with modest incomes would face a major hindrance if there were an inflexible obligation to

provide a fixed amount of public interest legal service without compensation, and this will inevitably influence a determination as to whether our suggestions are realistic for adoption by the bar in a particular locality.

CHAPTER FIVE, PART B (Page 45) *Use the Active Voice*

Rewrite these sentences using the active voice and omitting surplus words.

1. If undue risk is to be avoided in your law practice, it must be remembered that attorney malpractice suits are becoming increasingly common, and ample malpractice insurance is regarded as a necessity by most prudent lawyers.

2. The jurors should be respected by attorneys, but undue solicitude should be avoided. An attorney's posture of fawning deference or attempts to curry favor are resented by jurors.

3. Within three days after a Preliminary Notice of Default has been filed by Owner, cancellation of all outstanding credit vouchers shall be made by Lender or Lender's agents.

4. Good faith efforts to purge the contempt by respondent shall be taken into consideration by the court when the sentence is set.

CHAPTER SIX, PART A (Page 49) *Word Order*

Rewrite these sentences to emphasize the term "malpractice".

1. The avoidance of malpractice is only one of the many good reasons for careful legal research by attorneys.

2. In suits for malpractice, a higher standard of care is required of legal specialists.

3. Public defenders paid by the state can be sued for malpractice by their indigent clients.

4.   Any person who was intended to benefit directly from the lawyer's services can in an action for malpractice be regarded as a foreseeable plaintiff.

CHAPTER SIX, PART B (Page 50) *Closing Gaps in Sentences*

Close the gaps in these sentences by moving the inter-vening words or by splitting one sentence into two.

1.   The principles of the radar speedmeters now commonly in use by highway patrol units as well as by metropolitan police forces are scientifically sound, yet problems in the form of equipment design limitation and operator error still exist.

2.   Essential to the use of radar speedmeter readings in court is a program of regular equipment testing.

3.   The result of failure to permit the radar unit to warm up a minimum of ten minutes will be inflated readings.

4.   Operation within the immediate vicinity of a radar unit of x-ray or diathermy equipment can also cause inflated radar readings.

5.   A speeding vehicle on a multilane freeway at a time of heavy traffic or amid an irregular background of build-ings, signs, trees, bushes, or the like, is difficult to single out on a radar speedmeter.

CHAPTER SIX, PART C (Page 53) *Modifier Problems*

Rewrite these sentences to solve the modifier problems. If a sentence has more than one possible meaning, select whichever one you wish and rewrite the sentence to ex-press that meaning without ambiguity.

1.   Being constantly alert for signs of mechanical or dynamic injury, the deceased is examined by the pathologist at the autopsy to determine the cause of death.

2. A skilled pathologist is able to distinguish between structural changes produced by trauma and those produced by disease through years of training and experience.

3. In gunshot cases, a determination must be made whether the wound was inflicted before or after death by the pathologist.

4. Because of lack of mass and velocity, the pathologist will usually have difficulty with projectiles fired by small calibre pistols.

5. A pathologist only can express an expert opinion on the probable cause of death.

CHAPTER SEVEN (Page 57) *Avoid Language Quirks*

Rewrite this passage to free it of language quirks.

It is important to bear in mind that the outside remunerative income-producing activities of the judge should be so limited that he will not be or seem to be affected by them in his decisions. Clearly, his judgments should be free from bias or the appearance of bias. In addition it should be noted that his extrajudicial functions and activities should be so limited as not to impair the public image of him as very much devoted to his judicial duties. For the latter reason there was a great deal of somewhat strong criticism of the appointment of Justice Jackson as chief prosecuting attorney in the Nuremberg Trials. And in the same respect, some newspaper journalists, as well as a few academically oriented professional legal educators, leveled very scathing rebukes at Chief Justice Warren for accepting the designation as chairman of the assassination investigation commission charged with inquiry into the murder which resulted in President Kennedy's death.

SELECTED BIBLIOGRAPHY

Little that you read in this book is new. Most of it has been said before, some of it many times. To acknowledge a few of my many debts to other authors, and to guide you in your further study of this subject, I offer this selected bibliography of the works that were the most help:

T. Bernstein, *Watch Your Language* (Atheneum 1976)

R. Dickerson, *The Fundamentals of Legal Drafting* (Little, Brown 1965)

R. Flesch, *The Art of Plain Talk* (Collier 1951)

H.W. Fowler, *Modern English Usage* (2nd ed., Gowers) (Oxford 1968)

E. Gowers, *The Complete Plain Words* (Fraser rev. ed.) (HMSO 1973)

J.C. Hodges & M.E. Whitten, *Harbrace College Handbook* (8th ed.) (Harcourt Brace Jovanovich 1977)

D. Mellinkoff, *The Language of the Law* (Little, Brown 1963)

W. Strunk & E.B. White, *The Elements of Style* (2nd ed.) (Macmillan 1972)

H. Weihofen, *Legal Writing Style* (West 1961)

INDEX AND LAWYER'S WORD GUIDE